Nothing To Say

by

Peter Newman

Edited by Pam Warren

First Edition Published 2009

All rights reserved. No part of this publication may be reproduced, stored in a retrieval system, or transmitted in any form or by any means – electronic, photocopying, recording or otherwise – unless the written permission of the publisher has been obtained beforehand.

Copyright © 2009 by Pamela Warren

ISBN 978-0-9556928-1-9

The moral right of the author has been asserted

Preface

After Peter's death in 2006 it was inevitable that we would fall into spells of re-reading his letters, prose and verse. Over the years he had written so much, for himself or for and to us, using different styles and formats.

Through his verse we can remember some very personal moments and be constantly reminded of his wit, intellect and eloquence. The verses are autobiographical and there are a number of family events recorded along with Peter's thoughts and feelings.

Prompted by comments from family and friends, I hope this book will allow his collection of verses a wider audience, which they surely merit.

In putting together this collection it was difficult to decide on the order; by date of composition, random, or grouped in some way. Opting for a random sequence allows for some light relief during some of his darker subjects. Also the three verses inspired by the Eastbourne and Hastings holiday towns can be separated, which possibly does them more credit. However, being consistent with the random order may well detract from a few subjects, specifically 'fatherhood'. For example, the verse on page 18 was written about a visit from his teenage son on his motor bike, a generation on from the boy on page 8.

It has also been difficult to decide on how true to remain to the original layout, style and punctuation. The majority of Peter's writing was done on a manual typewriter and it is tricky to know why certain grammar appears as it does - for example page 34 - his use of capital letters for Bingo and Cinema. In general he has been rather consistent sticking with lower case for new sentences and paragraphs. I have assumed a purpose from him and reproduced his punctuation and line breaks with only some minor exceptions. In terms of page layout I have introduced some variety easily achieved in word processing, which would not have been so easy on his old typewriter.

It may be worth noting that this is a large selection of the verses written by Peter, but not a complete collection. In addition he was a prolific letter writer, and devised much whimsical prose.

Inspiration for the title of this book has been slow in coming. I'd nearly given up and opted for something standard like 'Verses by....'; when, re-reading one of his satirical writings (a story about an author and interviewer) he uses the title 'Nothing to Say' for an award winning book of blank pages. Then came the flash of memory – it was a phrase he sometimes used. The more I thought about his written and spoken word the more I thought how apt his own title would be, I very much hope those who knew him would agree with a smile.

Pam Warren
nothingtosaypoems@yahoo.com

Contents

Verses
by Peter Newman   1 - 52

Alphabetical list of first lines   54 - 55

'Nothing to say'
by Peter Newman   57 - 60

❖ ⌘ ❖

Dry summer dust of earth in garden sheds
stirs childhood memory
of solitary games, day dreams with fantasy companions
which later, lead to conjured romance and other fancies
wed, not to the common ground or work, events and people
measuring out the mornings, afternoons and evenings
of my discontent

for years and months and weeks
with some particular days and mornings spent
in summers heat and winters chill, in factory labour
or walking went, through the village alleys
and the back streets of the town
frustrated, wasted days
wasted, tasted days

bookshops and cinemas and blundering fumblings in the dark
dreamlands oases
in the summer in the park and in the winter evenings
overcoated, wet with rain, seeking secret corners
to search and journey, it seemed in vain, taking for the moment
that pleasure, assuming this to be the measure
of life's treasure

little knowing, nothing seeing

those eagerly embraced, accidental courtings
mistaking fantasy and dreams of love for love
each one a misalliance
hurt or hurting
sometimes both
expecting fulfilment of some silly dream
woven from that flickering screen
and bookish high romance
disguising plain corporeal need, self deluding
flawed and faulted by the poverty of circumstance
and my ignorance

little knowing, nothing seeing
often wept

the fettered cages of the Sunday afternoons
with cups of tea and cigarettes and waiting
mark the passing hours
with ennui and an itch not understood
waiting for the cinema to open
there to lose in the close packed darkness, tranced
the memory of those days and days and days
a flickering compelling fiction suspending disbelief
reality enhanced, usurped, replaced
increased the alienation of my working days and ways

an affliction, a poverty of life
imagined people and events devoured and devouring
week after week, for months and years
withdrawn into a tangled scheme of dreams
furthering a natural indolence and masking
that inability to do, contribute and endeavour
conjure instead, familiar paths to easy content
cloaking in pretence that lonely meanness
of my existence

so much missed

one fading photograph in some lost album
     my only epitaph
          I did, I was, I am, all fast receding
               windows on uncertainty revealing
                   nothing .....

Life Span

Observe that fleeting figure
bounding fast
from hump to tousled hump
of uncut grass,
then on to asphalt, pavement
factory and office floor,
then carpet, woodblock
build, beget;
unflagging yet.

                        Ending in a doorway
                        doubled up with pain,
                        grotesque
                        this figure will not run again.

deserted factory

the darkened silent factory
was not yet silent, quite,
all activity had ceased
and those who worked at bench, machine,
long gone,
to home,
and social life.

the workshops creaked,
sound of machines
and metal cooling,
settling,
hot air duct whisper,
air lines dying hiss,

a faint warmth of
combined endeavour lingers
in the air
where so many worked together

works offices, planning, progress,
line the wall
deserted, open,
cluttered witness to
the days events.

distant automatic cisterns flush
one light left burning
for the cleaner
to aid dim eyes discerning
what product of the day
lay piled along his way

from office to office,
duster, broom and bag in hand
he progressed, emptying
and cleaning
ash tray, wastepaper bin
ready for the next days din.

❖ ⌘ ❖

They walked together down the street
each hand held the others,
the boy and the man
hand in hand,

the boy, once past a certain age
no longer seeks that hand,
the need diminishes
for that comfort and support,

and comes a shyness, a reticence
in touch, a curious distrust,
something unconsciously to be avoided
with the passing of the years.

this discomfort of the flesh
walls off and utterly destroys
the comfort that was there,
for both, the joys.

isolation follows, each from the other,
considered normal, so ignored.

the loss is not apparent to the boy
in growing, other things crowd in upon
the mind, emotions partly hidden
partly forgotten,

re-emerge as comfort sought
in contact with the other sex
condoned, under the banner of loves pursuit
legitimate.

the father too, subject to the same taboo's
aware, vaguely, of a sense of loss
accepts, dismisses, seeing others
wishes no regret to feel

and then one day he sees,
walking down the street
each hand holding the others
a boy and a man
hand in hand

when ... suddenly ...
he cannot see for tears
and all those years

if they could only have it all again.

duck fly
head anticipating destination
stretches straight
against the morning sky

intent, intense,
wing beat, unhurried flight
and watched, breath stilled
till out of sight.

Bombing down the motorway on the annual holiday

Finger lickin' – lip smackin'
bottom stickin' – plastic padding
pre-wrapped
instant meals
for all you hurrying people on wheels.

One thousand good places for you to eat
      for less than the price of a cinema seat

the salmonella snack bars' glitter
beckons bike boys and baby sitter,
crowding to self servery
to rest awhile, and break the journey.

One thousand good places for you to eat
      for less than the price of a cinema seat

space invaders fill the entrance
incessantly advertising their presence
close by, the ever present malodorous mist
signals where the gents have pissed.

One thousand good places for you to eat
      for less than the price of a cinema seat

as a wise Chinese (I think) once said,
it is better to travel than to arrive
but then in his day,
they didn't have the motorway

Have we lost the game, my love?
starting at love all, we played
each point scored
and marked up on that unseen board

    not by the players
    but by circumstance and chance
    grinning on the side line,
    from me thine, and you mine

        to polite and civilised behaviour
        keep respectful distance, little said
        like relatives, to share
        a home; and bed

            having recourse now and then
            to habitual embraces,
            the last remaining traces,
            in gesture

                of that communion
                that once fired and bound us
                colouring all thought and action
                ending in sad separation

Today I am incompetent,
do not ask me
today,
to put up shelves
mend leaking taps
or fuses,
or anything else that stubbornly refuses
to function,
my stars are in the wrong conjunction.

and so we make our beds

and so we make our children's beds

they stood, the gate between
he on one side
the children on the other
this moment not foreseen

the boy turned away, not looking
yet not moving
the girl stood, watching
no word speaking

did his irresolution show
he wondered,
and wondered
at his own surprise

in seeing how irrevocable this act
this parting, betraying
knowing regret, and regret pointless
stood motionless

struck suddenly with loss
wishing to undo, retract, retrieve, go back
to as it was, as it had been
he wished

and wished
and, being younger
wondered what they wished
knowing instantly pretence

he knew

had always known,
and knew, the planning of this act
this separation, handing over and withdrawal
blindly ignored that wish

in confusion, shame
he turned to go, it seemed
stupidly and unforgivably
the only thing to do

and so we make our children's beds

I am

hand held high, I cry
I am
am I? what am I?

caucasian, anglo Saxon, fifty six
hurriedly cast into this fix
of self evaluation

ambitions, never
desires, plans, schemes, extending ever
only to the passing pleasure
or ease of work, responsibility and care

this mote flashed briefly
in the blaze of mans history
purposelessly,
entirely negatively

except for issue

and even they seemed hardly of my doing
no blood, sweat, tears or pain
did I contribute for that gain
was I deserving?

that two such can result from eagerly sought
and momentary pleasure
contains no justice

where then, and to whom
do I turn in gratitude?

I can but thank their mother, and them
for they are of their own making
and in that making, bestow on me
mysterious, unforeseen and unmerited content

my life, by them given purpose, and well spent

He arrived while I was out
the bike parked at the kerb
on my return, stood stark

      a lean machine,
      no fairings, tricks, embellishments
      a silent weapon, parked

           we talked a while of this and that
           desultory, disconnected chat
           we're out of touch, no matter

                gathered on the pavement,
                the scream of that machine
                in going, stops the heart

He couldn't get it on the bus!
and the conductor said,
consulting his handbook for:-

'Fare assessments for unusual, large, and extraordinarily large objects'
that he couldn't find a precedent
that would enable him to assess a fare anyway.

He had precise instructions, or
good guidance, on charges for:-

Folding push chairs
ditto deck chairs,
perambulators
and parts of escalators,
drum kits, pop groups, prize marrows
and billiard cues, (with or without balls)
gold fish, caged birds
and various herds, of cattle,
Siamese twins
and several other things,
boa constrictors, pet camels
and hippopotami.

but nothing to cover a contingency
like this !

He suggested, grinning, we try Pickfords
and rang his bell,

Ding ! Ding !

two weeks by the sea

They sit in rows behind the blazing glass
isolated from sea breezes and the sun
and all activity upon the beach, gazing
at the glittering sea, each year they come

from guest house and hotel converging
each morning and each afternoon
to sit in that curved concrete shelter
fall to sleeping, sitting, waiting

for the evening when they return
to guest house and hotel, to eat
gathering at the bar and seeking
other, fat upholstered seating

hasn't it been a lovely day, they say
soon to rise to leave the room, taking
cigarettes and glasses to the TV room
settling into other chairs, watching

mutter polite greeting and reply
soon be time to go to bed, where
wrapped in Dunlopillowed sleep, they wait
for breakfast in the morning

of bacon, sausages, eggs, tomatoes, toast
marmalade and tea, then walk down
through town, toward the sea
to sniff the air, then claiming

their chair behind the blazing glass
where, isolated from the sea breezes and the sun
and all activity, they read romances
for a while, then fall to sleeping, waiting

In sleep I keep awake
that memory,
and with remembered dream
I warm myself each day.

Your presence in your
absence grows.

The Survivor

Good fortune will not be so kind or able
to arrange, that we should die
together at the breakfast table,
or in bed, our goodbyes said.

one will remain
to wander through that empty house
occasionally cleaning,
and sometimes fall to dreaming,

of time past, a loss;
try not to feel the present state
will daily rise, to nothing; rather late

read papers, books ceasing to engage
all intercourse become intrusion
to the silence of the lengthening days.

THE SEASIDE TOWN

The unlit poster plastered Bingo hall
is not seen by that rheumy eye
that passes by
each afternoon.

Each afternoon ….
joined by a morning and a night
of ennui and small ritual
performed mostly out of sight.

Echoed by the boarded windows
their eyes unseeing gaze, turned inward,
as together and alone they bridge
the chasms of the days.

Slippered journeys to the corner shop…
small purchases are made,
sometimes to sit unnoticed
on the rusting promenade.

These neglected and neglectful, in their
one rooms and their flats
make tea and open biscuit tins
filled with photographs.

Creased fragments, held trembling;
remembering ....remembering,
dimmed eyes bent close, recapturing,
moments from the past.

Of children ....children,
lost children of their youth
adult now and never seen,
find sad comfort in remembered dream,

Of those young arms that once ....
those cheeks ...those eyes...that glance
round corners spying;
games in summer sunshine spun

Laughing, breathless, as the race begun
long gone for them;
all slowly dying...
to the constant chorus of the seagulls' crying.

a remembered death

They found him in the morning,
in the kitchen,

wedged in between the cooker and the sink.

a small man, slumped, shrivelled,
by that last pain
and death
and all that life inflicted.

armchair and bed an irritation
he sought a harder refuge, standing.

at what exact time I wonder,
in the darkness of the night
had he, blindly shuffled
to that room.

did he think,
of all those years .....and years,
and years.

and were there tears .....

or,
no thought at all,
all blotted out,
with wordless feeling
leaving, only
a constant agonised appealing,

oh God …..dear God …..please God,
please.

and finally,
in death,
did realisation come
that this unsatisfactory life was done.

❖ ❖ ⌘ ❖ ❖

I am itch,
not Ilyavitch Pyortr Ilyavitch
my Russian cousin,
nor brother to that nasty bitch
psoria-sis,
a simple itch am I.

which,

afflicts daily all humanity
yet am not noted in verse or song
by anyone,
not even that prolific Donne
neglecting me
in preference to the flea.

I seek attention.

the time has come
for recognition
of my effect on your condition.

If my existence is not commemorated
soon,
in print, I shall,
by dint
of extra work
increase the labours of the scratch
no match,
for me.

Guitar Envy

The masturbatory guitar
raised rampant
marks out the rhythm for
the crowded chant,
the phallic microphones'
bulb tip, caressed with lip.

soiled button vest and grubby jeans
a necessary adjunct to the headless screams
across the stage they
stamp and strut
in the conception of
animals in rut.

they would make the microphone
to cream, or even dribble
with a splutter,
and with one long, last,
ejaculatory scream
lost in the crossing laser beam,

fall exhausted to the floor
unzipped
undone
unmanned
and hopefully.
unheard of
any more

❖ ❖ ⌘ ❖ ❖

he stood,

searching with eyes to see
beneath the skin, inside the skull,
behind the eyes
of that face staring at him
from the mirror

what kind of man was that.

the eye regarding him showed no emotion,
no thought, nothing.
nothing could be seen,
or guessed at.

he lolled his head to left
and right, an inert puppet on the wall,
he grinned.
the eyes remained expressionless,
revealing nothing.

stretching his mouth wide
skin tight, eyes wide, he glared.
glare returned glare, impassively,
seeing nothing but distortion.

relaxing, he resumed his search,
the mirrored eye regarded his
without curiosity, his eye
must reveal no curiosity.

no way of telling what sort of man that was.

a thought occurred ..... discomfort.

no way for either of them
to tell what sort of man that was.

reality considered image, and
image considered reality,
each and both found nothing.

the image disappeared
and reality went down to breakfast.

both dissatisfied.

he poured a cup of tea, and thought,
perhaps the image goes off somewhere
and has breakfast too.

he hesitated.

or was he the image.

he hurried from the room
went racing up the stairs
into the bathroom, and there,
there in the mirror was the image,
where it should be.

he sighed with relief.

and then, hesitated.

which one am I

am I looking into the mirror
or out of it

which side of the mirror am I on

reality and image cleaned their teeth,
reality with a right handed right hand
the image, with a right handed left hand.

reality left the bathroom and
walked slowly down the stairs.

the image remained in the mirror
closely examining his teeth and
idly wondering, what sort of man am I,

and who on earth is that chap who
keeps on dashing in and out of the bathroom.

Splash wet, crack black
the broken pavements pass
stained crumbling houses
in wastes of uncut grass.

fenceless,
windows boarded,
keep from public gaze
the neglect of poverty and age.

no need avert the eye,
pretend;
nothing to offend
or cause discomfort

to indifferent crowd,
jostling to the promenade
and rusting pier
intent on Bingo, Cinema and beer.

plastic tables in cafes
reflect the neon glare
where space invaders bleeping;
unceasing, rend the air

❖⌘❖

your presence
is in me,
surrounds
encloses
inhabits
possesses

obsesses

                    I do not even wish to break
                    the bond

                    yes I do

                    or am I my own gaoler?

                    where's the key?

Loss

the tear fell
or was suspended,
the flawless surface held
all it reflected

another followed
so was movement
and source,
that saw
lingered,
turned inward

the eye .....

whose eye .....

in liquid contemplation
of what might have been

my eye

unmoving
transfixed,
looking at the thought of

your presence

A Lament for my Mother

In this chair – she sits
its fettered comfort brings no ease
for she would stand and walk
barefoot upon the sand and grass
and run

but has become
confined by infirmity and age
locked in with fitful unquiet memory
journeying at random around her head
troubling her with thoughts
of those long dead

and sons

and sometimes can but cry
soft music from another room
a long familiar little tune
a line of song – a word
and then those tears do gently come
and run.

For the young man with Temporal Lobe Epilepsy

As if by the wet chuckling sound of a brook
I could call up its memory and know the life of water.

As if by the moist loamy smell of a sod
I could bring forth its possibilities and know the life of earth.

As if by the warm gentle touch of a summer breeze
I could rise to soar with the wind and know the life of air.

As if by the glowing vision of burning embers
I could light some vast passion and know the life of fire.

And through the mystery of my quantum mind
know the universe
and feel its touch.

❖ ⌘ ❖

hair gummed
to beaded forehead
bedclothes
tumbled

limbs entwine
convulse
like pulse

symbol
outward sign
of that other

communion

I humbly beg

Idle thoughts prompted by listening, once more,
to the whole of La Boheme.

Why do we seek this searing sadness?
is there deep within
some element of gladness?

Are those tears not tears of anguish
after all?
that unchecked down our cheeks
so quietly fall.

Tales of unrequited love, unrealised bliss,
true happiness denied,
untimely deaths provide.

Sad endings, that release emotions
lying buried; now we glimpse,
and feel again

that inner strand of pain
to the passion and affection
of being loved and loving,

discovered and experienced once,
(it cannot daily be sustained)

This tragic story so poignantly unfolding
renews what then we had when holding,
each other

now conscious of that intermittent temporary loss
reminded of the utter gladness
mingling with the sadness.

of loss and gain,

loss and gain.

a seaside retirement

the windows looked out to
the glittering sea,
we made ourselves a cup of tea
and wondered what we should do next,
and next.

cushioned yes, but isolated
feeling suddenly, most cruelly
castrated.

trying not to remember things gone
friends, acquaintances,
familiar places.

is this now how it will be,
for me and thee,
just cups of tea
and walks along the prom.

to sit and wonder in the
westering sun,
what else in life we might have done,

what else we might have done.

Fuzz, Fuzz, Fuzz, Fuzz,
waiting in the lay-by
bored and cramped
and constipated
all day long they've sat
and waited,

sat and waited

not for crime or
misdemeanour
not for flashers self exposure,
not for rape,
not for theft,
not for murder,
not for mugging,
or masked raiders down the street
come running.

sat and waited,
constipated.

just to catch somebody out

sat and waited

over zealous admonishers
like school monitors,

odd socks,
slack laces,
tie askew
we're just waiting to report you.

catch 'em out
been waitin' long enough

better spot a young'un
wiv long 'air
better still if there's a pair
in some old banger
swerving on the ice

catch 'em out

there goes one now
silly little bugger, lets 'ave 'im smart
show 'im what it's all abart

stop the car and
check the steering,
brakes and winders,
the boot, the tyres,
the bleedin' fenders.

anything will do my son
just so long as we pin one
on you.

been waiting long enough.

breathe in this 'ere bag my lad,
watch it changin' colour;
pretty i'n it, that'll do
down the station now for you,
down the station
for verification
of your degree of intoxication.

while 'es in there,
thank Christ for that!
we can go an' 'ave a crap.
Gawd I didn't 'alf need that.

just got time to 'ave a cuppa
then wiv luck we'll catch anuver.

Heart and Mind

I

Twixt intellect and emotion
there is no chasm
for in each
the other finds
fertile soil.

The intellect stretches
and laterally finds
its understanding
of all emotion.

And emotions now
so clearly known
by both heart and mind
may freely bloom.

The beast set free
by trust of knowing mind
can at last
give its all

II

The heart is no longer subject
to the taxonomic, reductionist logic
of an intellect developed apart

they have grown together like twins
and guide each other

the intellect likes to simplify
whilst the heart likes to complicate.

The country House

Objet d'art, the bric-a-brac of ages
chipped plaster casts, dark paintings
the library, and arid acre
of cracked spines and yellowing pages

bought by the yard to dress the room
and man, seeking to impress
uncut unread; now mouldering
alongside the pretender, long dead

small groups wander through the rooms
where bare boards creak at each foot fall
and ever watchful matrons – Pringle clad
stand unobtrusively against a wall

and seem glad to answer all enquiries
for events and generations long gone
who had in those rooms slept
now in undisturbed silence kept

a great forbidding four poster bed
draped, canopied and counterpaned
looks frayed and grubby, slightly stained
and, in another – another bed

later, almost tumbled down a stair, where
in one dark corner, having tripped upon a board
I stood and grasped a swinging cord
that did service as a rail and nearly fell

carefully to the ground descending
then through a heavily studded door
joining an orderly and unimpatient queue
waiting – another room to view

and last, a small tea room with kindly ladies
dispensing tea in beryl ware
where muted conversation fills the air
and I am grateful for the chair

Observations on a recent wedding
(in the manner of Ted Hughes)

being unemployed and having nothing better to do
crow perched, feet cold, upon the gilded spire
head cocked, one beady eye downcast, observing
carriages, procession, crowds give way and sway
toward the building he supported

brazen trumpet fanfare made him blink, recalling
hunger, his polished beak twitched down, intent
no chance of a worm down there, he thought,
spat one glistening arc and, flew away
the building stirred, a small tremor
registered.

      or perhaps better still-

      wedding - ? said crow, what wedding - ?
      farted and flew away.

The Roué's regret

Lost opportunities, lost chances
traded for those passing glances

each new surrender and possession
bestowing, in receiving
ego's most coveted prize
to be desirable in desirable eyes

discover and disclose
approve and be approved
each day, rapturously renewed

the chase masks the passing time
with stealth converts to passing years
then suddenly, alone with fears

unanswered

Idle thought number six

I think the world is totally odium

give me a large whisky and sodium

Alphabetical list of first lines

page/s

And so we make our children's beds	14-15
As if by the wet chuckling sound of a brook	38
Being unemployed and having nothing better to do	50
Dry summer dust of earth in garden sheds	1-3
Duck fly	10
Finger lickin'- lip smackin	11
Fuzz, Fuzz, Fuzz, Fuzz,	43-45
Good fortune will not be so kind or able	23
Hair gummed	39
Hand held high, I cry	16-17
Have we lost the game, my love?	12
He arrived while I was out	18
He couldn't get it on the bus!	19
He stood	30-33
I am itch	28
I think the word is totally odium	52
In sleep I keep awake	22
In this chair – she sits	37
Lost opportunities, lost chances	51
Objet d'art, the bric-a-brac of ages	48-49
Observe that fleeting figure	5
One fading photograph in some lost album	4
Splash wet, crack black	34

The darkened silent factory	6-7
The masturbatory guitar	29
The tear fell	36
The unlit poster plastered Bingo hall	24-25
The windows looked out to	42
They found him in the morning	26-27
They sit in rows behind the blazing glass	20-21
They walked together down the street	8-9
Today I am incompetent	13
Twixt intellect and emotion	46-47
Why do we seek this searing sadness?	40-41
Your presence	35

Inspiration for the title of this book came from the following whimsical piece – one of Peter's many :-

Peter Maximilian Wolfgang Newman was born on Wapping Old Stairs (third tread up from the bottom) in 1926, shortly after this the family moved to Lower Effing-Likely where he attended the local Lycee until he was expelled in 1932 (for gross interference with gym slips). He continued his studies at the feet of the Mahatma Veeraswami Veeralynn; majoring in chiropody and graduating Alpha Sigma cum lordy-lordy in 1965.

He is internationally famous for his no novels; gaining world wide critical acclaim and the Bluebell prize for literature in 1972 for his monumental no novel 'Nothing to Say' and the Fitzwilliam-Hoofer award for his mammoth trilogy 'Nothing More to Say' in 1978.

He now lives with his mistress Ulla Thoebensen the Danish author, playwright, actress, chanteuse, ballet dancer, opera singer, Olympic weight lifter and civil engineer in the Downlands Guest House in Bristol. They have gathered around them a coterie of pseudo intellectuals and the general ambience is reminiscent of the Algonquin Hotel in down town New York in the late 1930's. The place is knee deep in tattered copies of Comic Cuts, the Wizard, Hotspur, Lilliput, Penthouse and The Rupert Bare Annual. The Rupert Bare Annual is a Homosexual publication and not to be confused with the children's book based on the adventures of a character named Rupert Bear.

Our interviewer is Algernon Y Peabody of the Avant Guard Railway Engineers Review and Chard Parish Magazine.

The interview took place during the summer of 1982.

The author, Peter Maximilian Wolfgang Newman is wearing a Hawaiian shirt and a pair of shorts that made our interviewers eyes water. Throughout the interview Mr Newman smoked a twenty four inch long, black Russian cheroot; frequently stopping to cough, spit and wipe the tears from his eyes.

In order to get the interview going; so that ' we can all relate like' as the author put it; he asked Ulla, his phemale pheeder of phallic phantisies to mosey on over to the bar and collect a tray full of stingeroos. She came back saying 'shit – shit- shit' (she pronounced it shit). 'This sure is one helluva dump' she said, ' no stingeroos for christsake; whadayawanna come here for anyways?'

'Relax', the great man says 'whatsamaddawidyahoney? relax, will ya; so we'll have Horlicks. That ok with you young feller' turning to our interviewer. 'Oh sure, sure' says Algernon. So Ulla slogs it back over to the bar to order the Horlicks. While she is gone the great man shifts uneasily around on his seat (he has piles) and says to Algernon ' well young feller, fire away; whadayawanna know'

Algernon asks:- can you tell us Mr er Newsome –er er- Mr Newcomes, your writing routine is ?, I mean, do you set yourself a daily quota of words? do you write in the morning or in the afternoon?; do you use a typewriter or a pen?. Our readers sure as hell would like to know.

Young man, said the author, I don't use a goddam typewriter and I don't use a goddam pen; or anything that makes a mark on the goddam virgin paper. It's obvious to me that you've never read a no book in your life; cause if you had you'd know there was five hundred or more blank pages; not a single word in 'em. What today's thinking reader wants is a no book. No story, no plot, no beginning, no middle and no end. No philosophical discussions on where's the best place in the house to put the john. No murders, no butlers, no upstairs maids; no death, no sex, no shooting, no sex, no robberies, and no sex; just nothing. The reason the intelligentsia love my work is they can sit down in their favourite arm chair, turn a page or two and go to sleep.

Me and Mr Ah-So, the chairman of the Mitsubashi-Kasawaki-Kamikasi Manufacturing Co are bringing out an automatic page turner in the new year. You can set the damn thing to turn the pages over at any rate you choose; depending on whether you're a fast or a slow reader. You can set the page turner going and go outside and dig the garden, paint the ceiling, sleep, go to the john, do your aerobics, anything you damn well please, and still get through the book ….

Don't get the idea, he continued, that writing a no book is peanuts, it aint. It takes a helluva lot a thinking about, a deal of time gathering all that no information and planning all the no action. I guess maybe my average time for a novel is about eighteen months. I cushtomarily (the Horlicks was beginning to take effect) work in the sheller; ish cooler down there an...............

Unfortunately. Our interviewer Algernon lost the remainder of his notes whilst changing trains at Sodding Chipbury. A priceless loss to posterity, and perhaps the reason why the interview has never been mentioned in the Paris review.

www.ingramcontent.com/pod-product-compliance
Ingram Content Group UK Ltd.
Pitfield, Milton Keynes, MK11 3LW, UK
UKHW041434180426
11947UKWH00007B/431